HOW TO STOP BEING TOXIC

By

NADIA HART

Introduction

Our relationships, mental health, and general well-being can all suffer from toxic behaviour. It can take many different forms, including hostility, criticism, or manipulation, and it frequently goes unrecognised or untreated. Toxic conduct must be identified and addressed in order to promote positive relationships and personal development.

We will examine the value of self-awareness in this tutorial as it relates to recognizing our own poisonous qualities and comprehending how they affect other people. Along with these topics, we'll talk about how to deal with toxic behaviour through self-reflection, therapy, support groups, and effective communication techniques.

We may overcome negative tendencies and build a happier, more contented existence by establishing healthy habits and making self-care a priority. Together, let's go off on this path of self-awareness and development as we work to create better relationships and put an end to destructive behaviour.

There lived a young woman named Maya in a charming little village. Although Maya was well-known for her vibrant personality and charisma, she also battled poisonous behaviours that frequently caused tension in her relationships with other people. She had a short fuse for criticism, was easily envious, and carried unfavourable ideas that soured her relationships with friends and family.

One day, Maya understood she needed to change after having an emotional talk with a close friend who was worried about her conduct. Determined to overcome her harmful habits and foster more uplifting connections, she set out on a path of introspection and development.

Maya acknowledged fisher problematic behaviours and their underlying reasons, delving deeply into her prior experiences and insecurities that had influenced them. She looked for self-help and therapy to work through these problems and create constructive coping skills.

Maya concentrated on increasing her sense of self-worth and confidence as she engaged in the process of self-improvement. She took care of herself, did joyful things, and surrounded herself with upbeat, encouraging friends who supported her development.

Maya made a deliberate effort to strengthen her bonds with other people while she focused on improving herself. She developed her ability to speak honestly and freely, using empathy and attentive listening to fully comprehend and establish connections with others around her. She accepted forgiveness and let go of her grudges. deciding to address disagreements with empathy and comprehension.

Maya's efforts began to show results over time. Her chats became more upbeat and pleasant, her presence emanate warmth and generosity, and her connections developed as trust and respect blossomed. She saw a transformation in her interactions with others.

Maya became a lighthouse of positivity and positivity in her community via her devotion to constructive relationship-building and self-improvement. She adopted an attitude of growth, compassion, and understanding instead of allowing poisonous thoughts and behaviours to cloud her interactions.

Maya shared love and positivity everywhere she went, encouraging others to follow in her footsteps as she went on her path. And by doing this, she not only brought harmony and fulfilment into the life of herself, but she also fostered a true community based on compassion, understanding, and camaraderie. Maya's tale thus turned into a testimonial to the transforming ability of growth, positivism, and self-awareness in overcoming negative behaviour and fostering meaningful relationships with oneself and others.

Therefore the contents within can neither be stored electronically, transferred nor kept in a database. Neither in part nor full can the document be copied, scanned, faxed, or retained without approval from the publisher or creator.

Table of contents

Chapter 1
Understanding toxic behaviour

There are many ways that toxic conduct can appear, and it can be detrimental to one's relationships, surroundings, and general well-being. Toxic conduct must be understood in order to be identified and appropriately addressed. When attempting to comprehend hazardous conduct, keep the following important points in mind:

Identifying toxic conduct: Toxic behaviour can take many different forms, including aggressiveness, manipulation, dishonesty, criticism, and controlling behaviour. Knowing these indicators can make it easier for you to spot harmful conduct in others.

Recognizing the root causes: Deeper emotional problems like insecurity, low self-esteem, or unresolved trauma frequently give rise to toxic conduct. It's critical to understand that toxic behaviour is frequently a mirror of the person's inner difficulties rather than always being an outright assault on you.

Setting limits: When handling toxic behaviour, it's critical to establish sound boundaries. This could entail establishing boundaries with people who display toxic behaviours or outlining precise expectations for your treatment.

Dealing with toxic behaviour: Although it can be difficult, it's critical to express how the conduct is affecting you in an honest and forceful manner. Having candid and open discussions can aid in laying the groundwork for change.

Getting help: Handling toxic behaviour can have a negative impact on your psychological well-being. It's crucial to ask for assistance from dependable family members, friends, or mental health specialists to help you get through these trying times.

Thinking back on your own actions: It's crucial to consider how you may have contributed to or allowed toxic dynamics in relationships. Toxic tendencies can be broken by being self-aware and receptive to criticism.

You may cultivate settings and relationships that are healthier and more positive for yourself and others around you by becoming aware of toxic behaviour and taking proactive measures to address it.

Importance of self awareness

Being self-aware is essential to identifying and dealing with toxic behaviour. Self-awareness is crucial in the process of ceasing to be toxic for the following reasons:

Toxic pattern recognition: Self-awareness enables people to identify the harmful patterns and behaviours they engage in. People who are aware of their ideas, feelings, and behaviours can recognize when they are engaging in harmful behaviour and take appropriate action.

Recognizing triggers: Self-awareness enables people to recognize the fundamental causes of the poisonous behaviours that result from them. Through identification of the feelings or circumstances that set them off, people can improve their ability to control these stressors.

Accepting responsibility: Being self-aware entails accepting accountability for one's deeds and realising how harmful behaviour affects both the self and other people. Having knowledge of the repercussions of their actions, people can actively endeavour to transform for the better.

Perspective-taking and empathy: People who are self-aware are more likely to be able to perceive things from several angles and have empathy for other people. This can encourage them to make amends by illuminating the effects of their poisonous behaviour on others around them.

Personal development: Self-awareness is the cornerstone of personal development. People can attempt to become more self-aware and make healthy changes to cease being toxic by reflecting on their actions, attitudes, and beliefs.

Seeking support and assistance: Part of being self-aware is realising when you need assistance and support to deal with harmful behaviours. Self-aware people are more likely to look for support groups, therapy, or counselling to address their harmful behaviours in a constructive way.

All things considered, self-awareness plays a crucial role in the process of ending toxic behaviour since it helps people identify, comprehend, and alter their negative habits. People can greatly advance in their transformation into happier, healthier selves by practising introspection, reflection, and openness to changes.

Chapter 2
Recognizing Toxic Attributes

Negative actions or personality traits that can negatively affect people and relationships are known as toxic qualities. Typical harmful characteristics include some of the following:

Manipulation: Those who are manipulative utilise strategies like gaslighting, guilt-tripping, or lying to get control over others. Self-awareness, introspection, and a deliberate attempt to strengthen relationships are necessary to put an end to toxic communication behaviour. Here are some tips to help you quit communicating negatively:

Engage in active listening,by concentrating on genuinely comprehending the viewpoints of others without interjecting or planning your reply, while they are speaking. Be understanding and affirm their emotions.

Refrain from criticising and placing blame: Rather than blaming others or levelling accusations, concentrate on utilising "I" phrases to communicate your wants and feelings. Say "I feel hurt when...", for instance, rather than "You usually give me the creeps."

Own up to your mistakes: Own up to the times you have acted in a poisonous way, and accept responsibility for the effects it has had on other people. Express sincere regret and pledge to make improvements.

Establish limits: Establish clear limits, with people and show respect for theirs. By doing this, miscommunications and disputes that can result in negative conduct are avoided.

Develop appropriate emotional regulation, by counting to ten, taking deep breaths, or, if necessary, removing yourself from the situation. Refrain from exploding or responding rashly.

Request feedback: Get frank assessments of your communication approach, from dependable friends or family members. Embrace constructive criticism, with an open mind and take advantage of the opportunity it provides, to get better.

Develop your assertiveness by communicating your ideas and opinions in an open, courteous, and straightforward way without being confrontational or submissive. By doing this, you can voice your wants without engaging in harmful conduct.

Practice self-care: Look after your physical, emotional, and mental health to lower stress and enhance your capacity for constructive interpersonal interaction.

You may quit communicating in a poisonous way, and create stronger, more meaningful connections by regularly putting these tactics into practice, and being aware of your actions.gain.

Jealousy: Being overly possessive and jealous can result in undesirable actions like following a partner about, claiming they are unfaithful, or cutting them off from friends and family.

Being extremely sensitive to criticism, always looking to others for approval, and having a poor opinion of oneself, can all be indicators of insecurity.

Passive-aggressiveness: Passive-aggressive people use subtle and indirect behaviours to convey their anger or resentment rather than confronting problems head-on.

Control issues: Individuals who struggle with control issues, may attempt to control or dictate the choices and behaviours of others, which can rob them of their freedom and autonomy.

Narcissism: Narcissistic people frequently prioritise their own needs, over those of others around them, have an exaggerated sense of self-importance, and lack empathy.

Toxic communication patterns include using harsh words, criticising others nonstop, and not paying attention to what other people have to say.

Refusing to accept responsibility for one's actions and habitually placing the blame elsewhere, is a poisonous behaviour that strains relationships.

It's critical to identify these harmful characteristics in both ourselves and other people.in order to deal with problems and strive for relationships and behaviours that are healthier and more positive.

Self-Evaluation and Introspection

Toxic behaviours in oneself must be recognized and addressed, and this requires self-reflection and examination. The following actions can assist in ceasing to be toxic:

Recognize and name poisonous behaviours: Give your acts and attitudes some thought. Tell the truth to yourself, about any poisonous habits you could be displaying, such negativity, envy, or manipulation.

Recognize the underlying cause: Examine the fundamental causes of your harmful habits. They may be influenced by taught behaviour, insecurities, or memories of the past.

Request feedback: Get frank comments about your actions, from family members or close friends. They might offer insightful opinions and viewpoints that you might not be aware of.

Develop self-awareness by observing your feelings, ideas, and responses in a variety of circumstances. Recognize when you are engaging in toxic behaviours and make an effort to determine what sets them off.

Develop empathy, by imagining yourself in other people's situations and making an effort to comprehend their thoughts and feelings. Gaining empathy can make you more sympathetic and understanding of other people, when interacting with them.

Set appropriate limits in your relationships to guarantee respect for one another and room for personal development. Setting limits can help stop harmful behaviours before they hurt you or other people.

Practice communication skills: You can get better at communicating, by learning how to listen intently, speak clearly, and handle disagreements in an amicable and courteous manner.

If necessary, seek professional assistance: If you are having trouble addressing and altering your toxic behaviours on your own, you might want to think about consulting a therapist. or advisor. They can offer you skills, support, and direction to help you overcome your poisonous traits.

Recall that changing harmful behaviours requires time and effort, and that self-improvement is a process. Treat yourself with patience, remain dedicated to introspection and personal development, and ask for help when you need it.

Identifying Toxic Behavior Patterns

Toxic behaviour patterns must be recognized, in order to identify and eliminate undesirable inclinations that endanger both ourselves and other people. The following are typical patterns to watch out for:

Persistent negativity: Relentlessly dwelling on the bad things that other people, circumstances, or even oneself have to offer may indicate toxic behaviour. Your perspective on life and relationships may be affected by this negativity.

Influence and manipulation: Toxic conduct may be demonstrated by attempts to exercise authority over others, influence circumstances, or control other individuals. Relationships that are imbalanced and harmful may result from this.

Lack of empathy: It is a harmful behaviour pattern to be unable or unwilling to comprehend and feel another's thoughts, feelings, and viewpoints. It may result in cruel deeds and a break in communication.regarding their sanity, reality, or recollection. It's critical to recognize this pattern in order to spot toxic conduct and safeguard oneself against emotional abuse.

Possessiveness and jealousy: Excessive feelings of possessiveness or jealousy in relationships, along with the controlling actions that follow, can be poisonous patterns that hurt the people involved as well as oneself.

Avoiding accountability: Toxic behaviours that impede personal development and harm relationships include avoiding accountability, offering justifications, or refusing to recognize the effects of your actions on other people.

You may address and modify these hazardous behaviour patterns by identifying them, and taking the appropriate action. It takes self-awareness, introspection, and a dedication to personal development to overcome harmful habits and promote positive interactions in relationships and conduct.

Chapter 3
Effects of Toxic Behaviour

Negative impacts on relationships and persons can result from toxic behaviour. The following are some typical repercussions of toxic behaviour:

Relationship damage: Tense, unpleasant, or even shattered relationships are often the result of toxic behaviour. Toxic connections can cause closeness to fade, communication to break down, and trust to be undermined.

Emotional distress: Emotions like hurt, rage, despair, and anxiety can be brought on by toxic behaviour. People who are subjected to toxic behaviours may suffer from low self-esteem, self-doubt, and emotional upheaval.

Effects on physical health: Prolonged exposure to toxic behaviour, can aggravate stress-related conditions, such elevated blood pressure, gastrointestinal disorders, sleeplessness, and weakened immune systems. The ongoing emotional stress can be detrimental to one's physical health.

Loneliness and social detachment: Toxic behaviour can cause social disconnection, and loneliness. Individuals that display poisonous tendencies, may be avoided by others in an effort to safeguard their own health.

Reduced productivity: Toxic behaviour at work can produce a toxic atmosphere that lowers motivation, morale, and productivity. It may also be detrimental to overall performance, team chemistry, and collaboration.

Reinforcement of negative patterns: Toxic behaviour has the potential to perpetuate harmful attitudes and habits, making it more challenging to stop destructive behaviour, and build better connections in the future.

Cycle of toxicity: Harmful and dysfunctional habits can be repeated from one person or relationship to the next as a result of toxic behaviour. The cycle might never end if awareness and action are not taken.

Legal repercussions: Toxic behaviour, such as harassment, abuse, or other misconduct, can sometimes progress to the point where it gives rise to legal repercussions. Serious consequences for one's personal and professional life may result from this.

It's critical to understand the consequences of toxic conduct, and to act proactively to address and alter these harmful practices. Toxic behaviours can be overcome and positive, rewarding relationships can be fostered, by seeking the assistance of mental health specialists, practising healthy communication and setting boundaries, and participating in self-reflection and personal development.

Effect on Partnership

Relationships can suffer from toxic behaviour, which can cause a breakdown in trust, communication, and general well-being of the parties involved. There are many ways that toxic behaviour can appear, including control, criticism, lying, manipulation, and emotional abuse. A healthy relationship's foundations may be threatened by these actions, which can produce a poisonous dynamic.

A breach in trust is one of the main consequences of toxic behaviour in a relationship. The other partner may find it difficult to trust their intentions and behaviours, if one partner behaves dishonestly or manipulatively, on a regular basis. This lack of trust can cause feelings of uncertainty and insecurity, as well as weaken the foundation of the relationship.

Toxic behaviour also has a significant effect on communication. It is challenging to have open and sincere conversation when one partner acts, in a dominating or criticising manner. In an attempt to take control of the situation, the toxic partner could try to cause miscommunication and animosity. This could start a vicious cycle of unhealthful communication styles, that ruins the bond even further.

The emotional health of both couples can be significantly impacted by toxic behaviour. Experiencing manipulation, control, or emotional abuse can result in depressive, anxious, or low self-esteem sentiments. Both partners' mental and emotional well-being may suffer as a result of the ongoing stress of managing a toxic relationship, which can result in a destructive cycle of dysfunction and negativity.

Toxic conduct in a relationship must be addressed, and it is essential that both partners understand and accept the toxic dynamics at work. In order to address underlying issues, and establish healthy communication and coping processes, this may necessitate going to therapy or counselling. The impacts of toxic conduct can be lessened and a more uplifting and encouraging relationship dynamic can be established by establishing boundaries, engaging in self-care, and placing a high value on respect for one another. Building a happy and healthy relationship ultimately takes dedication, work, and a readiness to adapt when dealing with poisonous behaviour.

Consequences for wellbeing and mental health

Relationship toxic conduct can have a serious negative impact on one's general wellbeing and mental health. The psychological and emotional well-being of individuals can be negatively impacted by any type of toxic behaviour, including manipulation, control, criticism, and emotional abuse. Toxic relationships frequently have the following negative impacts on mental health and wellbeing:

Anxiety and Stress: Managing a toxic relationship on a regular basis can cause elevated anxiety and stress levels. One's capacity to unwind and feel at peace might be negatively impacted, by a persistent sense of discomfort and hypervigilance brought on by a fear of conflict, criticism, or manipulation.

Low Self-Esteem: Relationship toxic conduct can erode a person's confidence, and sense of self-worth. Self-esteem can be damaged by continual control, manipulation, or criticism. cause feelings of inadequacy and self-doubt, eroding self-esteem.

Depression: Hopelessness, melancholy, and depression can all be exacerbated by being in a toxic relationship. Dealing with toxic behaviour, takes an emotional toll that might worsen pre-existing mental health conditions, or trigger the onset of depressive symptoms.

Isolation: People who are in toxic relationships may distance themselves from friends and family, in an effort to deal with the toxic dynamics, which can frequently result in social isolation. This may make you feel even more alone and alienated.

Physical Health: The emotional and psychological strain of a toxic relationship, can also have an effect on one's physical well-being. Prolonged stress can lead to a number of physical health problems, impair the immune system, and raise the risk of cardiovascular disease.

Cycles of Abuse: People who have been the victims of emotional or psychological abuse may exhibit a pattern of abusive behaviour, that is followed by regrets and promises to behave differently. This abusive cycle, can cause disorientation, guilt, and helplessness, which can exacerbate psychological damage over time.

People who are in toxic relationships must put their mental health and wellbeing first. This could entail deciding to withdraw oneself from the toxic relationship if required, setting boundaries with the toxic person, and asking for help from a therapist or counsellor. Creating a network of support, taking care of oneself, and participating in activities that enhance mental and emotional health can all help manage the negative impact of toxic behaviour on mental health. Never forget that putting your health first is crucial.

Chapter 4
Techniques of Communication

Self-awareness, introspection, and a deliberate attempt to strengthen relationships are necessary, to put an end to toxic communication behaviour. Here are some tips to help you quit communicating negatively:

Engage in active listening, by concentrating on genuinely comprehending the viewpoints of others, without interjecting or planning your reply while they are speaking. Be understanding and affirm their emotions.

Refrain from criticising, and placing blame: Rather than blaming others or levelling accusations, concentrate on utilising "I" phrases to communicate your wants and feelings.

Own up to your mistakes: Own up to the times you have acted in a poisonous way, and accept responsibility for the effects, it has had on other people. Express sincere regret and pledge to make improvements.

Establish limits: Establish clear limits with people, and show respect for theirs. By doing this, miscommunications and disputes that can result in negative conduct are avoided.

Develop appropriate emotional regulation by counting to ten, taking deep breaths, or, if necessary, removing yourself from the situation. Refrain from exploding or responding rashly.

Request feedback: Get frank assessments of your communication approach from dependable friends or family members.

Develop your assertiveness by communicating your ideas, and opinions in an open, courteous, and straightforward way without being confrontational or submissive.

By doing this, you can voice your wants without engaging in harmful conduct.

Practice self-care: Attend to your physical, mental, and mental health, to lower stress and enhance your capacity for constructive interpersonal communication.

You may quit communicating in a poisonous way, and create stronger, more meaningful connections by regularly putting these tactics into practice and being aware of your actions.

Engaging in active listening

One essential technique that can help stop toxic speech is active listening. Active listening improves interactions by showing the other person that you appreciate, empathise with, and understand them. Here are some pointers on how to quit becoming toxic through active listening:

Give it your all: When engaging in active listening, keep your attention on the speaker, and stay away from distractions like looking at your phone or planning your next move. Demonstrate your complete presence in the conversation.

Keep your eyes open: Maintaining eye contact shows curiosity and focus. It demonstrates to the speaker your interest in what they have to say and your level of engagement.

Employ nonverbal clues to your advantage. You might show that you are paying attention and comprehending the speaker by nodding your head, smiling, or bending forward. The speaker may be encouraged to continue communicating by these nonverbal clues.

Refrain from interrupting: Give the speaker space to share their ideas, without cutting them off. Await a moment before providing clarification or expressing your own opinions.

Think back: To be sure you understood what was stated, restate it in your own words. This demonstrates your active listening skills, and appreciation for their viewpoint.

Pose open-ended inquiries to elicit more details from the speaker, about their feelings and views. By doing so, you can demonstrate your genuine interest in what they have to say and help the conversation go further.

Demonstrate empathy, by acknowledging the speaker's feelings and attempting to understand their point of view. Say something like, "I can understand why you feel that way," or "That sounds difficult," to show empathy.

Refrain from making assumptions, about the speaker's experiences or emotions or from casting judgement. Be tolerant and accepting of those who have different beliefs and viewpoints.

You may promote understanding, stop harmful behaviour, and create better connections by integrating active listening into your communication style. Respect and affirmation are shown, through active listening, which fosters a more upbeat and nurturing setting for more healthful relationships.

Assertive speech

Establishing boundaries, and dealing with toxic behaviours in others and yourself can be done efficiently, with the help of assertive communication. Here are some pointers on using forceful communication to quit being toxic:

Acknowledge and recognize your harmful actions: Acknowledging toxic behaviours is the first step towards changing them. Consider your behaviours and attitudes that might cause harm or hurt to other people.

Accept responsibility for your actions: In order to change for the better, you must acknowledge, and accept your poisonous conduct.

Engage in active listening: When speaking with someone, try your best to pay attention to their opinions, and feelings. This demonstrates your appreciation for their opinions and promotes understanding between people.

Use "I" comments: Express your demands and feelings by utilising "I" words rather than by making accusations or placing blame on other people. Use phrases like "I feel hurt when you speak to me in that tone" as an example rather than "You always make me feel bad."

Establish clear boundaries: In order to safeguard your wellbeing, assertive communication entails establishing boundaries. Be stern while establishing your boundaries and make sure people understand them.

Ask for feedback on your conduct, and communication style from family members or close friends, and be willing to make changes. Accept helpful feedback with an open mind, and be prepared to improve.

Exercise compassion and empathy: Try to comprehend the thoughts and feelings of others in order to demonstrate empathy for them. Address conversations with rather than condemnation, and criticism, show warmth and compassion.

You can break harmful patterns, and build stronger relationships with those around you by using assertive communication techniques in your interactions and practising self-awareness.

Techniques for Resolving Conflicts

Approaches to conflict resolution can be especially beneficial in resolving harmful behaviours and promoting more positive relationships. The following tactics should be taken into account, when adopting dispute resolution to cease being toxic:

Remain cool and calm: It's critical to maintain composure and refrain from exacerbating a quarrel. Inhale deeply, then make an effort, to approach the disagreement with poise and serenity.

Engage in active listening by paying close attention to what the other person is saying and avoiding interruptions. Respect their opinions, and sentiments even if you don't agree with them.

Be forceful in how you communicate by using "I" words to clearly and non-confrontationally voice your demands and feelings. Instead than placing blame or accusations on the other person, concentrate on discussing how their actions have affected you.

Work together to find a solution: See the disagreement not as a war to be won, but as a problem to be solved. Collaborate to identify areas of agreement, and look into win-win solutions.

Accept accountability for your deeds: Own up to your part in the disagreement and accept responsibility for any harmful actions you may have taken. Express deep regret if required and promise to implement constructive adjustments.

Seek feedback and be willing to change: Show that you are eager to consider your actions, and are open to receive helpful criticism from others. Take the criticism as a chance to learn and advance yourself.

Set boundaries: To avoid future disputes and safeguard your wellbeing, clearly define your boundaries. Set and maintain consistent limits, by communicating them with assertiveness.

You may address toxic behaviours, hone your communication abilities, and create stronger relationships with others by employing these conflict resolution tactics. Any relationship will inevitably have conflict, but how you respond to it can greatly influence the atmosphere's ability to be constructive and peaceful.

Chapter 5
Defining Limits

Establishing healthy relationships and putting an end to poisonous behaviour require setting boundaries. Here are some pointers for successfully establishing boundaries:

Determine your own requirements and boundaries: Give it some thought as to what matters to you, and what actions you will no longer put up with. Recognize your own ideals and boundaries.

Make sure to express your boundaries clearly: Establish and communicate your boundaries with people in a straightforward and confident way. When communicating your demands and expectations, use "I" statements.

Maintain coherence: When establishing limits, consistency is essential. Set and enforce boundaries with consistency and without hesitation. People will appreciate and understand your boundaries if you do this. Make time for things that enhance your well-being and prioritise taking care of yourself. Having limits also entails being cautious. of who you are and honouring your needs.

Develop the ability to say no: It's acceptable to refuse requests or circumstances that don't fit inside your limitations. It's healthy to defend your principles and well-being by learning to say no.

Respect others' boundaries: It's critical to honour others' boundaries in the same way that you expect them to honour yours. Recognize their boundaries, and extend empathy and understanding.

Seek assistance: If you are having trouble enforcing or setting boundaries, get help from a therapist, family member, or trusted friend. They can offer direction, and support while you strive to establish more wholesome boundaries.

You can create a more positive dynamic in your relationships and stop harmful behaviours by establishing clear boundaries. Recall that establishing boundaries is a critical first step towards wellbeing and personal development. It is also a sign of self-respect and self-care.

Effective Boundary Communication

Setting and maintaining appropriate boundaries is essential to putting an end to harmful behaviour, and promoting positive relationships. Here are some techniques to assist you in politely and assertively communicating your boundaries:

Be precise and unambiguous: Express your boundaries in a direct, precise, and unambiguous way. Steer clear of confusing, or vague statements as they could cause miscommunications.

Employ "I" statements: "I" statements should be used to convey your wants and feelings when establishing limits. Say something like "I need some alone time to recharge" rather than "You never give me space."

Be resolute and self-assured: Maintain your composure and confidently express your boundaries. Don't apologise for establishing limits. since they are essential to your health.

Speak positively: When defining your boundaries, emphasise what you need rather than what you don't want. Say, rather than "Don't show up unannounced," "I appreciate it when you respect my time by giving me notice before dropping by."

Actively listen: By acknowledging the other person's sentiments, and listening to their point of view, you can promote open communication. This can promote respect for one another's boundaries and mutual understanding.

Establish repercussions: Make sure everyone knows what happens if they step outside of your boundaries. It is imperative that you carry out these consequences, in order to demonstrate your seriousness about upholding your boundaries.

Self-care is important. Make it a priority to look after your physical, emotional, and mental health. Establish limits. Recall that Establishing limits is a sign of respect and self-love.

Seek assistance when necessary: Consult a therapist, coach, or reliable friend for assistance if you run into resistance or struggle to express your boundaries. They can offer direction and support while you strive to establish and uphold limits in an effective manner.

Effective boundary communication helps you build stronger bonds with others, lessen conflict, and foster an environment that is courteous and upbeat. Recall that establishing boundaries is necessary to put an end to poisonous behaviours and is a sign of self-empowerment.

Chapter 6

Looking for Assistance and Encouragement

A critical first step, in kicking toxic behaviour and bettering oneself is asking for support and assistance. These steps will assist you in seeking, support and assistance if you realise that your actions are toxic and you want to change:

Acknowledge the issue: Recognizing that your conduct is toxic, and damaging is the first step towards getting treatment. Regarding how your activities affect both you and other people, be truthful with yourself.

Speak with a counsellor or therapist: A mental health expert can provide you tools and techniques, to assist you change as well as understanding of the underlying causes of your poisonous behaviour. Therapy can offer a secure, accepting environment where you can examine your ideas and feelings.

Join a support group: If you're interested in developing personally and improving yourself, think about joining a support group or community. Surrounded by people who are pursuing change as well can offer you accountability and support.

Speak with relatives, and trusted friends: Sharing your struggles with close friends or family members can also be beneficial. As you try to alter your behaviour, they can provide you with assistance, insight, and direction.

Become informed by reading books, articles, or going to workshops on emotional intelligence, communication techniques, and toxic behaviour. The more information you possess, the more capable you will be of implementing long-lasting improvements.

Engage in self-reflection by giving your thoughts, feelings, and behaviours some thought. To assist you, think about journaling or practising mindfulness. can aid in raising your awareness of the causes and patterns of your behaviour.

Establish boundaries: Acknowledge your limitations and establish boundaries with both people, and yourself. Make sure you express your demands in an authoritative, and unambiguous manner to stop other harmful conduct.

It takes time and effort to change toxic behaviour, so practise self-compassion and patience. As you travel this path, remember, to treat yourself with kindness and acknowledge your little accomplishments.

Recall that asking for assistance and support is a courageous, and proactive step toward healing and personal development. You are demonstrating your dedication, to become a better, more optimistic version of yourself by asking for help.

Counselling and Therapy

Counselling and therapy can be helpful tools for those who want to address and make changes in their lives. harmful habits of conduct. The following are some ways that counselling and therapy can assist in putting an end to harmful behaviour:

Finding the underlying problems: Whether your toxic conduct is the result of unresolved feelings, incorrect thought patterns, or experiences from the past, therapy can assist you in examining the fundamental causes of it. You can start addressing these underlying issues in a positive and healthy way by acquiring understanding of them.

Increasing self-awareness: Counselling offers a secure and encouraging setting in which you can examine your attitudes and actions. You may improve your self-awareness and comprehend how your activities affect both you and other people by engaging in self-reflection.

Acquiring new coping mechanisms: Counselling can provide you with behavioural, methods and coping mechanisms, to handle challenging feelings, and circumstances. By growing more wholesome methods, to manage your tension, rage, or fears, you can lessen the chance of acting in a poisonous way.

Developing assertiveness, active listening, and conflict resolution, are just a few of the communication skills that counselling can help you with. Effective and compassionate communication is a skill that can help you create happier, more fulfilling relationships, and avoid miscommunications that can result in negative behaviour.

Reframing and confronting harmful beliefs: Therapy can help you reframe, and challenge harmful beliefs or thought patterns that fuel toxic behaviour. You can develop a more positive, and realistic view of yourself and other people by changing your viewpoint, and thinking in more constructive and constructive ways.

Establishing and upholding boundaries: Counselling, can help you establish and uphold healthy boundaries, in your relationships. By becoming adept at making that stop you from acting in a domineering or manipulative manner.

Developing emotional intelligence: Effectively identifying and controlling your emotions, is a key component of emotional intelligence, which may be developed , with the use of therapy. Enhancing your emotional intelligence and self-control can help you react to difficult circumstances, in a more positive and understanding way.

Accountability and support: As you attempt to modify toxic behaviour, counselling offers a reliable source of accountability and support. In order to help you, stay on course and successfully, traverse the process of personal growth, your therapist can provide you with advice, support, and encouragement.

All things considered, therapy and counselling can be very effective tools for assisting you in ending toxic behaviour since they give you the knowledge, abilities, and encouragement you need to make life-improving decisions. Please do not hesitate to contact a certified counsellor or therapist who can provide you with the direction, and support you require on your path to self-improvement.

Community Resources and Support Groups

For those who wish to cease acting toxically, in their relationships and behaviours, with others, support groups and local resources can be quite helpful. These tools provide a judgement-free, secure environment where people can seek support, direction, and motivation in their efforts to overcome toxic behaviours. Here are a few instances of community resources and support organisations, that might help people with this process:

Professional therapy or counselling services have the potential to provide people the skills they need to identify the underlying causes of their harmful behaviour and devise plans to modify it.

Workbooks and self-help books: There Self-help books and workbooks addressing subjects, like conflict resolution, emotional intelligence, and communication skills are widely available. Those who want to stop, engaging in harmful conduct can find these resources to be a fantastic place to start.

Online discussion boards, and support groups: A plethora of online discussion boards and support groups are devoted to personal development, and self-improvement. Through these networks, people can interact with others who are going through similar circumstances, and exchange support and advice.

Workshops and seminars: Attending workshops and seminars on subjects like emotional control, empathy, and mindfulness can bring people, fresh perspectives, and practical tools to help them stop engaging in toxic behaviour.

Support groups for particular difficulties: For those coping with particular issues, there are support groups that might fuel toxic behaviour, like trauma, addiction, or anger control. Getting involved in a support group centred around these problems can assist people in addressing the underlying problems that might be causing their toxic behaviour.

Community centres and non-profit organisations: A lot of community centres and non-profit organisations provide resources, workshops, and support groups centred on interpersonal skills, mental health, and personal development. These resources can be a great way for those who want to stop their harmful activity to get support.

All things considered, finding local resources and support groups can be a critical first step in ending toxic behaviour and promoting happier, better relationships with others. People must always keep in mind that change requires time and effort, and that having a supportive community can make the path forward Making personal development more achievable and rewarding.

Chapter 7
Developing Good Habits

Toxic behaviour must be avoided at all costs by forming constructive habits. The following techniques, can assist you in changing your negative habits and mindset to more positive ones:

Self-awareness: Acknowledging your own destructive behaviour is the first step in ending it. Consider your words, acts, and thoughts for a moment, and note any activities that can cause harm, or hurt to other people. Recognize the negative effects your poisonous behaviour has on both you and people around you.

Develop mindfulness: Mindfulness enables you to be conscious of your thoughts and feelings as well as to be present in the moment. You can better manage your responses to situations and your own reactions by engaging in mindfulness practices, which can help keep toxic behaviour under control.

Empathy can be developed by placing yourself in other people's situations and making an effort to comprehend their thoughts and emotions. By fostering compassion and consideration, in your relationships with others, empathy can help you lower your risk of acting in a destructive way.

Set healthy boundaries: Preventing toxic conduct and preserving positive relationships depend on the establishment of sound limits.

It is important to express your boundaries to people in a clear and respectful manner. Setting limits aids in avoiding miscommunications and confrontations that may result in negative conduct.

Practice self-care: Keeping yourself emotionally, psychologically, and physically well is crucial to avoiding toxic behaviour, and keeping a good outlook. Schedule time for enjoyable and calming pursuits including hobbies, meditation, physical activity, and quality time with loved ones.

Seek assistance: Take care of yourself with uplifting influences, and ask for help from loved ones, friends, or a therapist if you find it difficult to give up harmful habits. When you're trying to break bad behaviours, having a support system can provide you with accountability, encouragement, and direction. Develop an attitude of appreciation by directing your attention, from your bad thoughts to your thankfulness for all the good things in your life. Gratitude exercises can foster a happier view and way of thinking, which lowers the chance of participating in harmful conduct.

You can cease being toxic, and develop a more positive and healthful attitude toward both yourself and other people by deliberately engaging in these behaviours and committing to your own personal development. Although it takes time and work to modify deeply ingrained behaviours, you may make positive adjustments and create a more gratifying and peaceful existence.

Take care of yourself

Self-care is crucial to ending destructive behaviours and promoting a happier, healthier mentality. Here are some pointers on using self-care to quit becoming toxic:

Consider Your Behaviour: Give some thought to what you've done and how it might have affected other people. Acknowledge any unfavourable behavioural patterns, and resolve to alter your behaviour for the better.

Set Boundaries: Toxic behaviours must be avoided by setting boundaries. Acquire the skill of communicating your personal boundaries in a straightforward and respectful manner.

Engage in mindfulness practices to increase your emotional awareness and self-awareness. Spend some time every day engaging in mindfulness exercises like meditation or deep breathing.

Seek Counselling or Therapy: Should you discover If you find it difficult to break bad habits on your own, think about getting counselling or therapy. A specialist can provide you techniques for implementing constructive adjustments as well as assistance in identifying the underlying causes of your poisonous behaviour.

Practice self-compassion: Show yourself love and forgiveness as you strive to improve yourself. You should show yourself the same kindness, and consideration that you would a friend.

Be Around Positive Influences: Assemble a circle of friends and family who uplift and support you, while you pursue your own development. Reduce the amount of toxic people, and situations in your life that can lead to bad habits.

Self-care Activities: Take part in enjoyable and soothing activities, such hobbies, physical activity, or time spent in nature. Taking charge of your mental and physical health is necessary to put an end to harmful practices.

Defy Negative Thoughts: Recognize when you are engaging in negative self-talk, then use positive affirmations, to counter it. Encouragement and self-compassion should take the place of self-criticism.

Develop Healthy Communication Skills: To enhance your communication abilities, try active listening, assertive self-expression, and understanding other people's viewpoints. Toxic conduct can be avoided by having effective communication, to help avoid misunderstandings and confrontations.

Celebrate Your Progress: As you strive to become a more upbeat and healthy person, acknowledge your little accomplishments and significant anniversaries. Recognize your accomplishments and keep working toward your own development and betterment.

Making Progress in Emotional Intelligence

Emotional intelligence development and the cessation of harmful conduct, require self-awareness, self-regulation, empathy, and effective social skills. You can avoid being toxic by following these tips:

Self-awareness: Know when you're acting in a poisonous way.

Self-regulation: Develop the ability to control your feelings and responses. Develop the habit of pausing, before reacting and consider the effects of your choices.

Empathy: Imagine yourself in other people's situations. Make an effort to comprehend their thoughts and feelings. By doing this, you can cultivate empathy and prevent harm to other people.

Social skills: Develop your ability to interact with others, and communicate. Develop your ability to communicate clearly and listen to people without passing judgement.

Request comments: Stay receptive to criticism of your actions from other people. You can use this to pinpoint your areas of weakness and begin modifying harmful behaviours.

Establish boundaries: Acknowledge and respect the boundaries set by others. This can lessen toxic behaviour, and foster healthy connections.

Engage in mindfulness practices, to help you properly control your emotions and remain, in the present moment. Additionally, it can assist you in raising awareness of your thoughts and actions.

Seek assistance: You might think about getting assistance from a therapist or counsellor if you are having trouble breaking poisonous behaviour, on your own. Guidance and resources to help you improve emotional intelligence can be obtained from professionals.

Recall that it takes time and effort to change hazardous behaviour. Practice self-compassion and concentrate on, implementing gradual, manageable adjustments in the direction of a better, happier outlook.

Chapter 8
Overcoming Negative Conduct

It can be difficult but essential to overcome harmful behaviour, if one wants to grow personally and maintain their wellbeing. The following tactics may be useful:

Identify and identify the harmful conduct: Acknowledging and recognizing toxic behaviour, is the first step towards changing it. This could entail considering your deeds and how they affect both you and other people.

Recognize the underlying cause: Look closely at the reasons behind your poisonous behaviour. Is it brought on by unfulfilled wants, fears, or bad memories? Addressing the underlying problems might be made easier, by determining the root cause.

Seek professional assistance: You may want to consult a therapist or counsellor, if you're finding it difficult to break free from toxic conduct on your own. They can provide you with useful information and resources. They can provide you insightful information and practical tools, to help you modify your habit.

Develop mindfulness and self-awareness by being conscious of your thoughts, feelings, and behaviours. By practising mindfulness, you can increase your awareness of your triggers and reactions, which will free you up to take breaks and choose better options.

Set limits: Overcoming harmful behaviour, requires setting boundaries. Say no when necessary, put your health first, and stay away from people or situations that exacerbate your poisonous inclinations.

Swap out harmful behaviours, for healthy ones: Look for more healthful methods to handle stress, control your emotions, and have productive conversations. Take part in enjoyable activities, such as hobbies, physical activity, or hanging out with encouraging friends.

If your poisonous behaviour has harmed others, own up to your mistakes and extend your apology.Sincerely apologise, and try to make things right. This might demonstrate your determination to change and help mend strained relationships.

Exercise self-compassion: It takes time and self-compassion to overcome poisonous behaviour. Take care of yourself, acknowledge your little accomplishments, and accept your mistakes when they happen. Recall that getting rid of poisonous behaviour is a process that requires patience and hard work. Continue to be dedicated to bettering yourself, ask for help when you need it, and have faith in your capacity to make positive changes.

Techniques for bringing about change

Although it can be difficult, changing toxic behaviour is undoubtedly achievable with the correct techniques and attitude. The following are some tactics to help you quit being toxic:

Self-awareness: Recognizing your poisonous habit is the first step towards changing it. Consider the potential harm that your actions may be causing to both you and other people.

Accept Responsibility: Own up to the things you've done and realise that you can make them different.

Request feedback: Consult with friends, relatives, or coworkers to get their honest opinions on your actions. This can give you important information about how other people view your behaviour.

Determine triggers: Acknowledge the circumstances or feelings that give rise to harmful conduct. You can deal with your triggers more proactively if you are aware of them.

Exercise Positive communication: To express oneself in a constructive and healthy way, work on honing your communication abilities. This entails speaking assertively, empathising, and actively listening.

Set boundaries: To stop toxic behaviour from developing, clearly define your boundaries with other people and with yourself. Observe the boundaries set by others.

Take part in activities that ease your tension, encourage happiness, and help you unwind.

Seek assistance: To address underlying issues that might be causing your toxic conduct, think about going to therapy or counselling. Talking to a reliable friend or joining a support group can also offer extra encouragement and support.

Swap out harmful behaviours for healthy ones: Determine which harmful behaviours, you wish to break, then swap them out for more wholesome ones. substitutes. Start engaging in constructive, gossip-free conversations, for instance, if you have a tendency to chatter.

It takes time and effort to change habits, so be persistent and patient. Continue to strive to be a better version of yourself and exercise patience with yourself.

Recall that change is a process, and making mistakes along the way is OK. It matters that you are dedicated to your own development and progress.

Managing obstacles and setbacks

Overcoming obstacles and disappointments can be particularly challenging if you are battling unhealthy habits or ways of thinking. While going through difficult times, consider the following advice on how to deal with poisonous traits:

Identify toxic behaviours: Acknowledging and recognizing toxic qualities is the first step towards overcoming them. Think back on your thoughts, feelings, and behaviours tendencies under difficult circumstances to find any poisonous behaviours that might be adding to your distress.

Face your negative self-talk: Be mindful of the words you use to describe yourself when you experience failure. Change your negative and self-critical ideas to more empathetic and upbeat ones. Remind yourself that mistakes and failures are a normal part of life, and cultivate self-compassion.

Ask for accountability and feedback: To get insight into how your actions might be affecting others, ask trusted friends, family members, or a therapist for feedback. Remain receptive to constructive criticism and make a firm commitment to improving.

Set limits: To safeguard oneself, from harmful influences, clearly define your boundaries in relationships and interactions. Saying no to people or situations that drain your energy is a skill. or encourage unfavourable ideas.

Develop appropriate, coping strategies to control your emotions when faced with setbacks. This is known as emotional regulation. Take part in relaxing activities, such journaling, exercise, meditation, or time spent in nature.

Practice self-reflection and self-care: Make self-care routines that support your mental, emotional, and physical health a priority. Make a schedule that incorporates your favourite things to do, including hobbies, working out, or hanging out with family and friends. Take advantage of quiet times for introspection and self-reflection to become more cognizant of your thoughts and actions.

Seek professional assistance if necessary: If toxic traits are really impairing your capacity to handle setbacks or if you're finding it difficult to break bad habits on your own, you might want to think about consulting a therapist or counsellor. Counselling can offer you the resources and assistance you require to deal with negative characteristics and create more constructive coping mechanisms. It takes time and effort to grow and change on a personal level, so be patient with yourself while you strive to let go of harmful habits and take steps toward a bright, healthy future.

Chapter 9
Preserving a Positive Relationship

Both partners must put in work and attention in order to maintain a healthy relationship. The following advice can assist you, in creating and maintaining a happy and healthy relationship:

Open and honest communication is essential to a happy and fulfilling relationship. Communicate your ideas, and feelings to your spouse in a clear and concise manner, listen to them, and work through any problems that may come up together.

Spend quality time with each other by going on dates, spending time in the kitchen strolling together, or just spending time together at home. Having shared experiences together makes your relationship stronger.

Trust: Establish trust by being dependable, truthful, and open with one another.

Respect: Be polite and respectful to your partner. Be aware of the effects of your words and deeds on people, and respect their feelings, boundaries, and ideas.

Support: Show your lover your presence in both happy and sad times. When necessary, provide comfort, encouragement, and emotional support.

Both partners must be willing to compromise in a relationship. Be prepared to compromise, make allowances, and come up with ideas that benefit you both. Preserve individuality:

Preserving your unique identities is just as vital as prioritising your partnerships.

Express your gratitude to your partner for all of their efforts on your behalf. Small acts of gratitude can make a big difference in fortifying your relationship.

Constructive conflict resolution is important since disagreements are a normal aspect of any relationship. When disagreements come up, handle them maturely and with the intention of coming to a mutually beneficial conclusion.

Seek professional assistance when necessary: Don't be afraid to ask a couples therapist or counsellor for assistance if you're finding it difficult to keep up a positive relationship. Expert advice can provide you with the resources, and resources required to improve your partnership.

You can keep your relationship healthy and enjoyable by putting communication, trust, respect, and support first and by being prepared to put in the necessary time and effort. Recall that while partnerships demand ongoing care and attention, the benefits of a solid, loving bond are incomparable.

Fostering a good rapport

Building solid and meaningful relationships requires fostering good connections with other people. The following advice can assist you in creating and preserving strong relationships with the people in your life:

Engage in active listening: Listen to people with genuine curiosity to see how they are feeling. This entails focusing, entirely on them, keeping eye contact, and posing meaningful questions to demonstrate that you are actively participating in the discussion.

Demonstrate compassion and empathy by making an effort to comprehend the other person's point of view and by acknowledging their emotions and experiences. Developing a stronger relationship, and a deeper connection with them can be achieved by demonstrating empathy and understanding.

Be genuine and open with others by freely sharing your ideas, emotions, and experiences. You may strengthen your relationship and gain their trust by being genuine and open with them.

Give thanks and appreciation: Give the individuals in your life your sincere gratitude and appreciation. Express your love and gratitude for them, as well as the great influence they have had on your life.

Schedule time for meaningful interactions: Devote time and energy to fostering your connections by spending meaningful time with the individuals you hold dear. This could be accomplished by engaging in activities together, having deep discussions, or just being in the same room as them.

Practice kindness and compassion: Be tolerant, helpful, and supportive of others in order to show kindness, and compassion. Little deeds of kindness can have a big impact on fostering a supportive and upbeat atmosphere and deepening your relationships with others.

Communicate honestly and openly: When you communicate with other people, be truthful and open. Strive to resolve problems in a courteous, and thoughtful way, and address any issues or concerns in an open and productive manner.

You may build solid, satisfying relationships that enrich your life with happiness, support, and purpose by heeding these advice and actively fostering meaningful connections with others.

Establishing Mutual Respect And Trust

Developing respect and trust in any kind of relationship—personal or professional—is essential to keeping a solid, and positive bond with other people. All meaningful interactions are built on trust and respect, and relationships can easily collapse in the absence of these two fundamental components. The following are some essential strategies for fostering mutual respect and trust:

Communication: Gaining respect and trust requires honest and open communication. Mutual respect and understanding can be fostered by actively listening to people and being open and honest about your opinions and feelings.

Consistency: Building trust requires being consistent with both your words and deeds. People will have faith in your credibility when you reliably fulfil your commitments and conduct yourself with integrity.

Empathy: Respect and a sense of connection are fostered by demonstrating empathy and compassion for the thoughts and emotions of others. Building relationships based on your compassion, for other people and their welfare cultivates a good rapport and trust.

Establishing limits: Gaining respect and trust requires adhering to boundaries. It demonstrates your respect for people' autonomy and uniqueness when you set clear limits and honour theirs.

Being trustworthy: People are more likely to trust you when they see that you are trustworthy and consistent in your behaviour. Whether it's arriving on schedule for Being dependable, showing up on time for appointments or offering assistance when needed is essential to developing trust.

Forgiving and apologising: Gaining the trust and respect of people requires you to be willing to own up to your mistakes, extend your apology when called upon, and extend forgiveness. Everyone makes mistakes from time to time, but how we respond to those mistakes can have a big effect on how strong our relationships are.

Appreciating people: Being thankful and appreciative of others fosters a sense of respect and acknowledgement. In each relationship, recognizing and appreciating the efforts of others creates a respectful and productive dynamic.

You may cultivate gratifying and significant relationships with others by implementing these behaviours into your interactions with them. Respect and trust are gained over time by persistently doing good behaviours, exchanges of ideas, and acts. Making these qualities a priority can help you build long-lasting relationships with other people.

Chapter 10
Accepting Personal Development

A journey of self-discovery and transformation, embracing personal growth enables people to realise their greatest potential. To attain personal development, one must be dedicated to lifelong learning, introspection, and moving outside of one's comfort zone. When embracing personal development, keep the following important factors in mind:

Self-awareness: Being self-aware is the first step toward personal development. Think about your objectives, values, beliefs, and areas of strength and weakness. Gaining a deeper understanding of who you are will enable you to pinpoint your areas of improvement.

Goal-setting: Make sure your objectives are attainable, consistent with your values and aspirations. Establishing SMART goals, specific, measurable, attainable, relevant, and time-bound, will provide you with a path for your own personal development.

Learn and pick up new abilities: Never stop learning and developing your abilities. This could be accomplished through self-study, online classes, workshops, or traditional schooling. Learning new abilities might increase your self-assurance and present you with more growth prospects.

Go outside your comfort zone: Taking chances and venturing outside your comfort zone are common components of personal growth. Accept difficulties and have an open mind to trying new things, even if they make you uneasy. Here is where learning and true growth occur.

Ask for feedback: Don't be scared to ask for advice from others, including dependable friends, coaches, and mentors. Positive criticism can give you important insights into your areas of improvement. and expand.

Take care of yourself: Growing personally involves more than just reaching success on the outside. It also entails looking after your physical, mental, and emotional needs. Schedule time for self-care pursuits like physical activity, meditation, hobbies, and quality time with close friends and family.

Accept setbacks and failures: Growing involves inevitable failure. Consider setbacks as chances to learn and get stronger rather than as indicators of failure. Having a growth attitude and accepting your mistakes might help you learn important lessons and advance yourself.

Honour your advancement: Celebrate and acknowledge the advancements you achieve in your quest for personal development. No matter how modest your victories may seem, be proud of them and use them as fuel to keep going.

Accepting one's own evolution is a lifetime commitment. a procedure that calls for commitment, introspection, and a readiness to change. You can reach your full potential and lead a more contented and significant life by making a commitment to your own development and remaining receptive to change.

Constructing a happy life free of toxicity

It's a path to create a happy, toxic-free life that involves introspection, boundary-setting, and surrounding yourself with supportive people. The following actions will assist you on this journey:

things like working out, practising meditation, eating a balanced diet, getting enough sleep, and taking up enjoyable hobbies.

Establish boundaries: Recognize the situations, relationships, or behaviours that are toxic for you and set boundaries to keep them out of your life. Saying no to things that don't benefit you properly will help you to put your own wants and wellbeing first.

Be in the company of positive people: Look for connections and settings that encourage and inspire you. Embrace the company of friends, family, and coworkers who inspire you to be your best self.

Develop an attitude of thankfulness by concentrating on the good things in your life. To change your viewpoint and discover happiness, in the here and now, keep a gratitude notebook or simply think back on the things you have to be grateful for.

Give up harmful habits and viewpoints: Determine whether harmful attitudes or actions are preventing you from leading a happy life. Contest these notions and make a concerted effort to conform to a worldview that is more empowered and optimistic.

Take part in meaningful activities: Look for things to do that will make you happy, fulfilled, and give you a feeling of direction. You can feel more satisfied and well-being when you participate in meaningful activities, such as volunteering, taking up a hobby, or achieving a particular objective.

Seek professional assistance when necessary: If you are having trouble overcoming negative behaviours, relationships, or emotions on your own, you might want to think about getting in touch with a therapist or counsellor. They can offer you methods, support, and direction to help you deal with difficult circumstances and build a more satisfying life.

Recall that living a happy, healthy life free of poison is an ongoing process that calls for self-awareness, dedication, and hard work. By being proactive and setting priorities for yourself, if you take care of your health and surround yourself with positive people, you may create a life that makes you happy, fulfilled, and at peace.